There's a Hole in My Chest

There's a Hole in My Chest

Healing and Hope for Adult Children Everywhere

William J. Jarema

Illustrations by Pat Mullaly

A Crossroad Book
The Crossroad Publishing Company
New York

The Crossroad Publishing Company
370 Lexington Avenue, New York, NY 10017

Copyright © 1996 by William J. Jarema

Cover art and illustrations by Pat Mullaly

Printed in the United States of America

Library of Congress Cataloging-in-Publication Data

Jarema, William J.
    There's a hole in my chest : healing and hope for adult children
everywhere / William J. Jarema ; illustrations by Pat Mullaly.
        p.   cm.
    Includes bibliographical references.
    ISBN 0-8245-1572-2 (pbk.)
    1. Adult child abuse victims—Life skills guides. 2. Adult child
abuse victims—Mental health. 3. Parenting. 4. Mentoring. 5. Self-
esteem.   I. Title.
RC569.5.C55J37 1996
616.85'82239–dc20   95-51046
                                                              CIP

Contents

Chapter 1

I Have a Hole in My Chest

HAVE YOU NOTICED that no matter how much you try to make yourself feel better, it never seems to work? Do you try to fill yourself up with work, helping others, food, sex, alcohol, or drugs and still have an empty space inside of you? When someone compliments you, does it seem to leak quickly out of you? After having sex, do you feel empty and still long for intimacy? After you have worked hard and know in your head that you have been successful, do the good feelings last for only a few brief moments? Do you feel that in the middle of your chest there is a heavy, dark, empty sensation that nags you, especially when you are alone? Have you tried to find fulfillment in prayer, religion, and spiritual quests and still feel that nothing seems to make you feel better?

Have you tried to fill that emptiness with all sorts of relationships, activities, and feelings/emotions, with spending money, buying clothes, or owning expensive things and yet realized that the sense of fulfillment lasts only a moment?

If you can say yes to any one of the above questions, you most likely have a hole in your chest. If you say yes, maybe this book can help.

Chapter 2

How Did I Get a Hole in My Chest?

AT BIRTH each child has a special, empty place in his or her chest. This space is empty so that the child can receive necessary life skills from both mom and dad. When mom and dad properly place the essential ingredients into the child's ready-made place, that place becomes filled, and the child becomes wholesome — not perfect, but wholesome and able to live a happy, productive, balanced life. This person — the empty space now filled with mom's and dad's contributions of these life skills — is then able to manage the complexities of life for the rest of his or her years. But what happens if either mom or dad or both don't give a child these life skills? The child still has an empty hole in his or her chest. This hole in the child's chest gets bigger, darker, more ravenous, and more powerful. This condition leaves the child with a lifetime of wanting and hurting, driven to fill this space with other things that usually don't work.

The Absent-Father Syndrome

Some people have a hole in their chest because their father was absent. Some dads may be absent because of separation or divorce. Some fathers were absent because they were not emotionally available or they were abusive physically, sexually, or verbally. Some people experienced the absence of their father because he was so wounded that he could think and feel only for himself. A dad like this is usually one who himself had a hole in his chest.

Some dads were absent because alcohol, drugs, work, power, or money became their best way to fill the hole in their chest. If your dad had a hole in his chest, then he probably didn't have the life skills needed to help fill the hole in your chest.

Our dads give us very special skills that help to fill part of the hole in our chest. Because our fathers have a biological blueprint that makes them male, they alone can impart certain life skills that we need to fill the hole in our chest. Our fathers help to fill the hole in our chest by teaching us how to manage, defend, compete, hold on to, protect, conquer, and provide.

These skills teach us how to make a "container." This container allows us to create boundaries, to set limits, to hold on to those things that we value. With a sturdy container we can defend ourselves, manage feelings and emotions, store memories, exclude harmful forces, and protect those things that are precious to us. Without a container, we are unable to manage feelings and emotions, defend ourselves, take a stand, make a commitment, make decisions, compete, or resolve conflict.

Some of us may have been given only a small

Mom's Fluid

embody
emote
relate
connect
touch
bond
affiliate
express
attach
include

Mom's
Fluid

Dad's Container

manage
contain
set boundaries
limit
defend
protect
compete
hold on to
provide
conquer
exclude

Dad's
Container

container, or the container we received from our dad may have a crack in it. What happens then? No matter how much good stuff you put into the container, it just leaks out.

The Absent-Mother Syndrome

Some of us had an absent mother because she was hurt and wounded by life. Our mom could not give us what we needed because she didn't receive life skills from her mom. Because of your mom's pain or busyness, she couldn't help fill the hole in your chest. It could be that the hole in her chest was so empty and hurting that she didn't know how to help you with the hole in your chest.

Sometimes moms are hurting so bad that they

drink, take drugs, overwork, overextend themselves, and excuse their husbands from helping with providing for some of the needs that we had as children. Some moms may actually not have been with us because of separation, divorce, or death. Some moms who may have been with us physically were anything but mothering. If mom was verbally, physically, or sexually abusive, then you may not have had a chance to be mothered. The space in your chest may not have been filled with the proper things that you should have received from her. If your mom has a hole in her chest, you may have experienced her as unapproachable, untouchable, and distant. Your mom's emotional distance may have left you guessing and wondering if something was wrong with you. Maybe you even felt that you were defective or damaged in some way.

Our moms give us some very special life skills. Because of the biological blueprint that makes her a female, mom imparts to us the ability to connect, to relate, to feel, to bond, and to include. Moms in particular give us the gifts of embodiment and affectivity. It's our mother who gives us what we need to be able to receive, to express, to belong, to relate.

Our mom gives us the fluid of life that we hold in the container that we get from our dad. A container without mom's fluid leaves us wanting, longing, pining, and yearning, uncomfortable with feelings and emotions. Without mom's fluid we are unable to bond and belong or to create friendships. We lack imagination, creativity, and receptivity. We may feel uncomfortable with intimacy and trust and with our bodies. We may not feel secure with ourselves and in relationship with others.

Chapter 3

Trying to Fill the Hole in My Chest

A s human beings we are built by God to love and be loved and to feel worthwhile. The non-negotiables of life such as eating, drinking, sleeping, breathing, and excreting are the bare essentials of life. Is there to be more? Yes! Each of us is made in God's image and likeness and has been designed to "live life to the full" — a promise that cannot be achieved alone. The longing for intimacy, the desire to be known by a significant other (belonging), and the vulnerability to let others know what you know (trust) are all signs of a longing to enhance our quality of life through close relationships.

All people need to be intimately connected to others so as to discover who they are, who they can become, and what they can achieve. The initial layer of our personal foundation for personal growth and development is laid by our parents. Without their unique contributions we are left without the resources that we need to promote that growth and development. The empty space left unfilled by our parents creates a hunger that demands to be filled. If mom and dad don't provide us with those initial life skills that help us to become intimate, to belong and trust, then anything second-best begins to look good. We try to use second-best intimacy, leftover affections, and short-term nurturance to fill the hole in our chest. Yet because these are only second-best, we have to keep getting more of these low-quality life experiences, creating an endless cycle of more-is-not-enough and enough-is-never-achieved.

The stories that follow illustrate well what happens when you try to fill the hole in your chest with second-best, leftover, and short-term fixes. The first step to breaking these dependent and addictive cycles is to name the emptiness, confess it out loud to a significant other, and then begin to establish *second-chance-mother* and *second-chance-father* relationships that will heal the hole in your chest.

Jacob works for a construction company. He is married with four children. His wife tries to build him up by telling him what a great guy he is and what a great father he has been to their children. Jacob says that he can't let anyone inside of him. He desperately wants to feel like he belongs and is connected to someone. Yet he keeps everyone, including his wife and kids, at a distance. Jacob says that he is often praised by his boss as being one of the best workers in the company. However, he can't seem to accept the compliments. He has received a few raises because of his outstanding performance, but he feels he isn't really worth it. Jacob recounts, "I hear the words of praise, encouragement, and gratitude, but I can't hold on to them for more than a few moments. Any good words or compliments seem to evaporate as soon as they touch my ears. I have spent most of my life looking for praise from others.

Yet when I get it, I don't believe it. When I want it, I'm afraid to ask for it. Why can't I let the affection and appreciation inside of me?"

•

Linda says that she has never been able to defend herself. "I'm so quick to apologize, excuse others, and let them off the hook. I'm driven by my own fears and get trampled over by those who want what I have. I shudder at the thought of competition. I never take a stand and speak my own opinion. I constantly have these conversations in my head about what I think and feel, but the words never get to my mouth. I'm such a wimp. I look inside of me and realize that I have no power, no self-value, and no self-esteem. There is such a chasm of emptiness inside of me."

•

Stephen is a successful manager at a grocery store. He has been dating a variety of women. Each time he is with someone on a date he tries to enjoy himself, but sooner or later, those empty, nagging feelings of loneliness, detachment, and withdrawal begin to consume him. Stephen says, "I know how to fake having a good time. I'm great with small talk and can put on a good show. But those feelings of emptiness drive me to end the evening as soon as possible. I usually come up with some excuse to get home. When I'm home, the loneliness becomes even worse."

•

Alice remembers that for most of her life she wondered what it would be like to be happy for more than just a few brief moments. She says, "I would like to know how not to sabotage myself from experiences of happiness. Anytime I am having a good time I prepare myself for the worst. I seem to feed off of this dark hole in my chest. I bring that darkness to just about everything I do. My friends have nicknamed me the Daughter of Doom. Even in the brightest moments, I begin to think and ponder negative and toxic ideas. Then the sadness takes over, and I have doomed myself."

•

Brian has been "high" on life for most of his adult life. Brian's wealthy family always provided Brian with all of the material things he needed or wanted. Brian tells the following story: "When I couldn't buy things to make me feel happy, I would get my happiness from drugs and alcohol. If I wanted to fill myself with great ideas and hopes, I would get stoned. If I was angry and couldn't get rid of the bad feelings, I would get drunk. If I wanted to be cool and become the life of the party, I would drink and drug. I just couldn't seem to access those feelings and emotions from within. All I ever felt inside of me was an empty space. I was so afraid, so terrified, to look inside this empty space. I thought that if I did look inside this empty hole in my chest, I would fall inside this canyon and never get out."

•

Tammy's story involves food. "My whole life has been designed around food. If I were feeling down and out I would eat milk products. If I were mad at someone, I ate crunchy cookies. If I were lonely,

I would eat chocolate. Any kind of chocolate would do. Food became my medicine for all of life's problems. I became an expert on what food could provide which feelings and emotions. I had a dream one night that turned me around. I was at the edge of a big hole. I was shoveling huge amounts of food into this hole. I realized that it was food that I personally liked. Then from a distance I saw myself shoveling mounds of food into my chest. I was trying to fill this hole in my chest with food. I woke up feeling really sick to my stomach. I realized it was time to deal with the real issue in my life: How did I get this hole in my chest?"

•

Judy says: "I don't know how to relax. I don't know how to just hang out. I don't have the vaguest notion of how to play. I have been the little adult my whole life. I came out of my mother's womb and began house cleaning. From the moment I was born I was told to grow up. I did! Today, I don't know how to play. I don't know how to have fun with simple things like walking in the park barefoot or trusting that when I walk the beach I won't need to stop and clean the beach. I never had anyone teach me how to hang out and have fun. Anytime I try to have a good time and play with friends, I am filled with anxiety and guilt."

•

Jack says: "Since I can remember, my whole world has revolved around my zipper. I was taught by my sexually abusive father that sex was the answer to all of life's problems. I was sexually active when I was nine years old. Since then, I have tried to fill the gaping hole in my chest with sex. I don't mean just your ordinary sexual activity. I have tried it all. I have been with men and women and multiple partners. Each time after sex, I would only have a few precious moments when I thought I was fulfilled. Then, the feeling of wanting and longing and hoping would begin again. I hoped that the next person I had sex with could fill that dark, empty space inside of me. It hasn't happened yet."

Chapter 4

Healing the Father Wound

THE LEAD TITLE of the June 1993 issue of *Time* reads: "Fatherhood: The Guilt, the Joy, the Fear, the Fun That Comes with a Changing Role." The title suggests just how important fathering is. However, although the U.S. Census Bureau can document the seventy million mothers age fifteen or older in the United States, it has scant idea how many fathers there are. "There's no interest in fathers at all," says sociologist Vaughn Call, who directs the National Survey of Families and Households at the University of Wisconsin. "It's a nonexistent category. It's the ignored half of the family." Studies of young criminals have found that more than 70 percent of all juveniles in state reform institutions come from fatherless homes. Children from broken families are nearly twice as likely as those in two-parent families to drop out of high school. Some psychologists suggest that boys without fathers risk growing up with low self-esteem, becoming overly dependent on women and emotionally rigid. As children get older, fathers become more and more crucial in their physical and psychological development. Researchers have found that children whose fathers are involved in their early rearing tend to have higher IQs, perform better in school, and even have a better sense of humor.[1]

Second-Chance Fathers

So what do you do if you missed out on these life-giving exchanges between yourself and your father? How do you retrieve what you lost or never got from your dad? Are you doomed forever to waste away and gnash your teeth for the personal damage done to you by the lack of a giving father? The good news is this: you can get all of the fathering life skills that may be missing in your life! What you need to do is begin to heal your father wound. Where to begin?

You begin by first admitting the absence you have felt between you and your father. Recognize what skills you are lacking as an adult that you should have learned from your father. Then tell your story to a significant other. This can be your therapist, best friend, spiritual director, next-door neighbor, or a close brother or sister. Once you are able to name the life skills that you are missing, then begin your search for a male who you believe can help you practice, experience, and master those life skills you need. Get yourself a second-chance father.

A second-chance father is a male person who can teach you some of the life skills that your father never imparted to you. He can be your sibling, grandfather, uncle, teacher, coach, next-door neighbor, co-worker, therapist, spiritual director, peer, or clergyperson.

If you are ready and willing to begin to create or strengthen your container, then find a man who can help you learn the life skills you need to own and integrate in order to begin to heal the hole in your chest.

In *The Grown-up Man,* John Friel reminds us, "Please don't trap yourself into a life of misery by saying that you didn't get what you needed from your father when you were little so you are doomed forever. Remember, you can get the fathering you need from any healthy man who is able and willing to give it. In some cases, you can even get it from someone who is younger than you."[2]

A second-chance father does not have to be older than you. He may impart to you only one life skill, and that could be the end of your relationship. Some second-chance fathers last a lifetime, and you may become lifelong companions. Some second-chance fathers will be men who may not have been good fathers to their own children. Yet a willingness to let them provide for you or impart some of their experience and knowledge can empower and transform these men. Most men who become second-chance fathers realize that the relationship is a mutual healing experience.

As we said earlier, when people don't receive from their parents the life skills meant for that special place in their chest, they live with an aching, hurting, empty, and wanting feeling. They can't be comfortable with themselves or with others and eventually even with God. They are handicapped by what has become a hole in their chest. Some people will try to fill the hole in their chest with one or many relationships, approval, religion, food, drugs/alcohol, work, success, money, anger, or control. These things will provide temporary relief, but that doesn't heal the hole in their chest. It doesn't heal the wound that can be inflicted only by a father, the damage that only a father can do.

Stories of Second-Chance Fathers

Janet has no fond memories of her father. She remembers, "My dad was such a critic. He made me feel so stupid about everything in life. I got married just to escape my dad and ended up marrying a man just like my father. After our third child, my husband left me. I attended a workshop where

I first heard of this idea of a second-chance father. I have two wonderful friends who are married and live next door to my home with their two children. We take turns babysitting and helping each other out with car pooling.

"I could always hear my father's negative criticisms echoing in my head telling me I couldn't do anything right. I was even afraid to pick up a screwdriver. I realized that I was always afraid of fixing broken things in the house. I asked my next-door neighbor's husband if he would consider being my second-chance father. I told him that there were three rules to this working relationship: (1) I don't want to have sex with you; (2) I don't want to be your friend; and (3) I want you to teach me things that my father never took the time to teach me. I said I wanted to be able to ask him to show me how to manage repairs in my home, manage my check-book, and begin to take charge of the upkeep of my house. Jack, my next-door neighbor, agreed to be my second-chance father.

"One day my lawnmower broke down. I asked Jack to come over and help me fix it. He showed me how to take each part of the engine apart and look in a manual to figure out what was broken. I did as he instructed me. I then went to the store to purchase the items that needed to be replaced. I came back and put the lawnmower back together. I started the lawnmower and it worked. I realized that with a little instruction and direction, I could learn to fix a lot of things. And I did! My second-chance father gave me just enough encouragement to help me see that I could learn how to conquer that broken lawnmower. I could manage the simple instructions that Jack gave me, and I could struggle with this new challenge and come out a winner. This newfound esteem has given me the courage to begin repairing all sorts of things in my home. After a year or so, I had read and studied many home improvement books. I also studied different manuals for lawnmowers and found that I had a knack for mechanics. One day Jack's riding lawnmower broke down. He pulled it into my garage and asked me to help him fix it.

"I took the challenge and within a few hours I had repaired the riding lawnmower. Because of my second-chance father, I have learned how to provide for myself, how to complete and conquer a task at hand, and how to manage new information and skills."

•

Jim can't remember having any playtime with his dad. He remembers his father always running late to work and coming home late at night. Jim is thirty-two years old and is really uncomfortable with any kind of sports. He met Sam, who is twenty-four years old, at a church event. Sam was trying to get a team of men and women to play softball. Jim said he would come to watch. He was too embarrassed to admit that he didn't know how to play softball. At the first scheduled Sunday afternoon softball gathering, Jim went to watch the others play. Sam met Jim and threw him a baseball glove and said, "Come on, let's play catch and warm up."

Jim was horribly embarrassed to admit that he had never thrown a ball in his life. Sam figured out pretty quickly that Jim didn't know his knee from his elbow when it came to softball. Sam showed Jim some of the basics of the game. They both took the outfield and stood close to one another so that Sam could coach Jim.

As the summer days passed along, Jim realized that Sam was more of a father to him than his own dad had ever been. Soon Jim trusted Sam and began to call Sam his "outfield father." Later in the summer Jim had a chance to ask Sam about sports and life in general. Even though Sam was younger and didn't have all the answers to Jim's questions, he and Jim talked long and hard about all kinds of things. Jim realized that he could manage a new event like softball. He even learned that he was pretty good at softball. This gave him the courage to try other sports. Jim now had a second-chance father to whom he could ask questions concerning how to compete and how to manage and conquer challenges. Jim's newborn confidence gave him a better feeling about himself, which has allowed him to take on new experiences and greater risks.

·

Mary's dad was a couch potato. She says, "My dad's sole contribution to my life was, 'Take it easy Mary, don't sweat over it.' I have no idea what it means to be on time, organize my life, make choices, grab for the future and make it happen, take a risk, think the impossible and make it happen. I'm forty-eight years old and find myself unable to move up in my career as an assistant secretary at a construction company. I'm one of eight secretaries in the company. I've been there the longest, twenty-two years, and I receive the least amount of attention or credit for the work that I do. The joke at the company has been that I couldn't find my way out of a paper bag. Why would I? My dad said, 'Don't sweat it!' Well, one day I went to buy a book for my boss for his birthday. The book I bought was *Fathering the Next Generation.*[3] I read the introduction and my eyes fell upon chapter 12 and its title: "Second Chance Fathers." I bought two copies of the book, one for me and one for my boss. I learned that having a second-chance father involves a formal relationship with a male person whom you admire and believe could teach you about life. I thought about who I wanted for my second-chance father.

"I had always had a good relationship with the different foremen, who each had a crew of workers. I felt really comfortable with one of the foremen. I knew he was happily married and had older children. I told him about this idea of a second-chance father. He told me that he understood the idea of a second-chance father because he had had the experience. When Arthur was seven years of age, his father died in a car accident, and that's when his next-door neighbor, Mat, companioned him as a second-chance father. Arthur told me that his second-chance father kept him on the straight and narrow road. He said: 'Everyday, Mat would ask me, "What are your three goals for today?" If

I couldn't think of any, my second-chance father would give me some suggestions. He taught me a valuable life lesson: how to make choices and see them through. He taught me how to stay in the fight and work hard for what I wanted. He always reminded me that if you really want it, you have to sweat for it.'"

Mary went on: "When Arthur said, 'sweat for it,' I almost fell off my chair. I told him that most of my life had been determined by consequences and not choices. I didn't know that I had choices. So began my story with my second-chance father. Everyday, Arthur would come to my office, and we would talk about my three goals. In three months I had been promoted two times and was then offered the position of executive secretary. Because of my success,

I was offered a job in our main office, which was downtown. I don't see Arthur every morning now to review my goals. I do call him about twice a week to talk about what choices I'm making and how well I'm sticking to the fight. I've learned the value of sweat — sometimes mixed with tears. Arthur has been my second-chance father for almost a year now. I have never met his wife or kids. We have never had lunch together. We don't socialize. Yet this man has helped me hold on to my own power, my sense of purpose, my destination, and my realization that I can do it!"

•

Doug had just started a new job at a small business that distributes office furniture. He was on his first delivery to a large firm. Doug was very happy to have landed this job. He had lost many jobs prior to this one because of his drinking and drug taking. Mr. Thomas, the building manager, met Doug at the loading ramp. It was at their first meeting that Doug became aware of a powerful feeling between him and Mr. Thomas.

During the unloading of his first shipment of inventory, Doug and Mr. Thomas began to talk about Doug's new job. Doug remembers how happy he was and how proud he was of himself. He wanted very much to share his success with someone. Mr. Thomas, in his wisdom, seemed to have sensed how hard Doug had worked to arrive at this point in his career, so he listened to Doug's story. After Doug had completed his delivery, Mr. Thomas said to him, "Doug, I'm proud of you for your new career accomplishment. Come by tomorrow and we'll have lunch together to celebrate your second day on the job."

Doug has known Mr. Thomas now for six years. He still refers to him as Mr. Thomas because of the respect he has for this man. Since that time, Doug has visited with Mr. Thomas often. He defers to this older man in many of his career matters and explains that Mr. Thomas has given him a feeling of worth and importance. Mr. Thomas has brought Doug into his family to the point that Doug often refers to the Thomas children as his foster brothers and sisters.[4]

Chapter 5

Healing the Mother Wound

IS THERE SUCH A THING as a bad mother? What happens when mom isn't able to give to her child those life skills that only a mother can impart? Mothers provide us with the first human encounters of taste, touch, smell, and sound. Our mother most likely is the first person we gaze upon and the first person with whom we establish a familiar and safe reality. Skin to skin, we learn from our moms the sensuality of cold, warm, soft, and sweat.

In time, our first understanding of separation and autonomy will be established as we learn that mom can leave us and we will be all right. Through our mothers we learn to feel with our skin, touch with curiosity, discover many levels of pleasure, and have our basic needs met by a divine, godlike figure who holds the source of our early childhood hopes, fears, and dreams. She can be for us a "nourishing soul, sheltering body, fostering spirit."[5]

Second-Chance Mothers

Moms are the creators "of the special realm that belongs to children, a realm characterized by spontaneity, creativity, playfulness, fantasy, wonder, curiosity; emotional vivacity in place of conceptual abstractions; thought processes that overcome natural laws, or what often is called magical thinking and a magical sense of concrete objects and actions; history as legend rather than as factual past time; shyness and shame in place of mannered decorum; an eidetic imagination leading to easy familiarity with make-believe voices, faces, figures, and with animals and ghosts; rhetorical joy — hyperbole, singsong, alliteration, rhyme, onomatopoeic and apotropaic noises, story-sequences, and the love of story. All this in one word: imagination."[6]

Mother can either nourish our imagination with the fluid of life or offer us no drink for the soul. Mother can teach us how to access the streaming, flowing, and life-giving energies that come through that intimate touch known between mother and child, or she can leave us dry and parched, drawn to emptiness, and detached. "Without positive attachment [to their mothers], children grow up unable to trust anyone; they are fearful and constantly test the safety or danger of their environment."[7]

A mother wound can leave a child/adult wandering aimlessly in life looking for nourishment in all the wrong places. Where can you go for the proper nourishment? You can go to a second-chance mother.

A second-chance mother is a female person who can share with you some of the life skills that your mother never gave you. She could be your sibling, grandmother, aunt, teacher, coach, next-door neighbor, co-worker, therapist, spiritual director, peer, or clergyperson.

If you are willing to receive these life skills from your second-chance mother, then you can begin to heal the hole in your chest that was caused by a mother wound. Find a woman who can help you learn about the fluid of life and how to integrate these essential life skills into your life and begin to enjoy living to the fullest.

Dr. Grace Ketterman, in her book *Mothering: The Complete Guide for Mothers of All Ages,* writes:

In four decades of medical training and experience, I have seen only a few children who were severely lacking in mothering; they were tragically damaged individuals. But I have seen a growing number of children and young adults whose parenting was inadequate in some way.

Their mothers were not bad people. They simply had not received the kind of treatment they needed to be the mothers they wanted to be.[8]

A second-chance mother does not have to be older than you. She may impart to you only one life skill, and that could be the end of your relationship. The relationship with some second-chance mothers lasts a lifetime, and you may become lifelong companions. Some second-chance mothers will be women who may not have been good mothers to their own children. Yet a willingness to let them connect with you or share some of their experience and knowledge can heal and transform these women. Most women who become second-chance mothers realize that the relationship is a mutually healing experience.

Stories of Second-Chance Mothers

Bob tells the story about his mom and her struggle with drinking: "I have no memory of my mom holding me or touching me or asking me how I felt about anything. Today, I am addicted to sex. I have tried for years to feel my feelings by getting physically involved with a lot of women. I made a retreat and met Sister Mary Ann, who was one of the retreat team members. I was in her small faith-sharing group. I can remember her asking me about how I felt being loved by God. I gave her a blank stare, and she came right back at me. I so much wanted to know what it felt like to be loved by someone that I screamed at her: 'I don't know what it means to feel loved by anyone. Teach me!'

"Sister Mary Ann explained to me that my parents hadn't given me what I needed to live life to the full, so I needed second-chance parents. Without her saying another word, I pleaded, 'Then you be my second-chance mom.' She agreed! Sister Mary Ann told me that there had to be some rules for us to work well together. These rules would be: (1) she would not have sex with me; (2) she would not be my friend; and (3) she would teach me how to relate with others, tell stories about my feelings and ideas, and let me ask questions that I always wanted to ask my mom about women, relationships, and feelings. It has been three years since I have had my second-chance mom. I still struggle expressing my emotions. But I can admit that the hole in my chest, which was so heavy and dark, has become lighter and not so painful. I have become more disciplined regarding sex and have established some really good friendships."

•

Cheryl's mom was a classic placater. She helped everyone. She taught Cheryl that if she wanted to be happy in life, then she should live for others and put herself last. Cheryl bought into her mom's equation of life. Cheryl got married and had seven children. She explains: "My whole life was for my husband's and children's happiness. Because we always struggled financially, I would go without. I was a bit overweight and didn't take good care of myself. My clothes, no doubt, were a little out-of-date. A few years ago my husband had a serious heart attack. I had to get a job to support the family while he was recuperating. I was told of a job at a local grocery store. I applied for the job and to my surprise was hired. My manager is twelve years younger than I, and she has become my second-chance mother. I realized that I was out-of-date on just about everything. I asked at least a thousand questions a day, and Allysa, my manager, taught me most of what I needed to know. In time, I moved from stocking the cosmetic shelves to part-time checkout. I spent time with Allysa after work hours, and she gave me a crash course on checkout duties and procedures. She also helped me update my clothing, cosmetics, and even changed my hairstyle. Allysa has become a woman I would like to model myself after. We have discussed some of the ways I could establish healthier boundaries for work and home. I have come to respect my body and care for myself because I am worth it. I feel that I have come to love myself more and in return have come to rewrite my definitions of love for my children and my husband. I can admit that I have become a healthier and happier woman. I don't need to give myself away to please others and feel valuable.

"I have begun to fill this empty space in my chest with affection, respect, and friendship. Allysa has taught me that I am a good person who works hard, and I am willing to learn from my mistakes. One of the most profound impacts that this woman has had on my life occurred when she told me that I was an attractive woman. She pointed out some of my finer features and helped me take ownership of my own sensual beauty. I have no memory of my mother, husband, or anyone telling me that I had personal beauty. I'm coming to like myself more and more each day."

•

Michael remembers his mom as distant and emotionally cold. "I once heard from one of my mom's brothers that my mom was sexually abused as a child. I always thought that there was something wrong with me because my mom couldn't get close to me. I'm thirty-two years old and have come to mistrust women. I work in a clothing store and recently have befriended an older saleswoman. Mrs. Carpenter is married with four children. We have always been friendly but distant. One day while we were on break, she began to talk to me about her son who had been in a serious car accident. He was not expected to live. When she began to cry, I felt a real sadness in my chest. We began to talk about her feelings for her son. God, I wanted to be her son for just a moment. I wanted her to be my mom and talk about me with concern, warmth, and interest. I confessed to Mrs. Carpenter how much I envied her son. I told her about my mom and the emotional absence I have felt most of my life.

"Within the next few weeks, Mrs. Carpenter's son fully recovered. We began to share our lunchtime together. She thanked me for listening to her and said it was time for me to get some mothering. Over the past few years, Mrs. Carpenter and I have spent a great deal of talk-time together. She has helped me experience trusting, bonding, and believing in the kindness of a motherly figure. I have noticed that

I am more approachable and less fearful of people and relationships.

"I recently began dating a girl and have found myself asking Mrs. Carpenter for a whole lot of advice. She patiently reassures me, but most importantly, she pushes me to experience a deeper level of emotional honesty. She can read my body language quickly and challenges me to dig inside that deep well of feelings and emotions and pull out the expressions that need to be revealed. Mrs. Carpenter has become my second-chance in life. Even today, I have never called her by her first name. She remains that wise old(er) woman whom I admire and respect."

•

When Maggie was about four years old, she woke up one night and didn't know whose bed she was sleeping in. "I walked out into the kitchen and saw a strange man and woman eating breakfast together. I casually climbed up onto one of the kitchen chairs and asked, 'Where am I?' These nice people then explained to me that my mommy and daddy were taken to jail because they were fighting and that I would be living with them for a while. Every year I ended up in someone else's home because my mom and dad not only fought but they drank, took drugs, and stole from everybody. I have no fond memories of my mom. She was such a hard ass.

"I got involved in drugs and drinking and got pregnant. For some reason I decided to keep the baby and ended up in one of those pregnancy-aid homes. The housemom was about my own age of twenty-four. At first, we did not get along. However, I didn't get along with anybody. I was always looking for a fight. Sarah, the housemom, taught me by her behavior what it meant to be a friend. I watched her care for a lot of the women who were scared, confused, and needed a listening ear. One day the house was short on staff. Sarah asked me to help her with the intakes and some other work. As we worked together that day, I realized that Sarah needed me. Something came over me, and I got really scared. Sarah noticed my strange behavior, and we began to talk. In the end, what gave me the most relief was when Sarah looked me straight in the face and said, 'I will not leave you. I will not abandon you no matter how much of a bitch you try to be to me. You can't scare me away.'

"Sarah was with me throughout my entire pregnancy. She stayed with me during the very difficult birth. Sarah has become my life line for helping me make good choices for my new job and how to care for my new child. She has helped me to feel a part of something and someone. This past year I have become a housemom. I have come to realize that I too can commit to someone and something and not run from the feelings of belonging. Sarah has become for me a sacred person. I'm not sure if I believe in a loving God, but if I did, Sarah would be for me that part of God that is truly believable, holy, and good. I feel connected to Sarah and have let her into my wounded world. She has been the best mom I have ever had."

Chapter 6

Expect Marvelous Things!

WHEN THE STUDENT IS READY, the teacher appears. If you are ready to heal your father and/or mother wound, the "second chances" of life will surround you, even to the point of your tripping over them. It has been my experience that once a client or student of mine has been able to find a word or a name that captures their experience for them, they are well on their way to wholeness. Naming our experiences, especially our losses, provides half, if not more, of the healing we seek.

New definitions for men and women have provided new insight and momentum for diverse expressions of healthy mothering and fathering. Our new definitions and concepts of masculine and feminine are breaking the oppressive limitations that have for centuries hampered the creativity that is built in specifically to each gender. Our willingness to get back to the basics will help to generate a happier and healthier generation of men and women who will parent a generation of children who will be filled with light, joy, creativity, and — most of all — imagination.

Madelyn Hochstein did a survey of one thousand men to determine what characteristics they most admired in other men. Some of the characteristics and the percentage of the sample who saw them as most admirable are the following: dependability (88 percent); honesty (88 percent); having a good relationship with family and friends (83 percent); making lots of money (18 percent); being high-powered (20 percent). The top five concepts for men today: emphasis on their own definition of success, not somebody else's (64 percent); a focus on fitness (59 percent); a deemphasis on material success (58 percent); a receptivity to new technology (57 percent); and a need for personal gratification over money at work (56 percent).[9]

The new male is emerging as a person who seeks balance and proportion within his life, work, and relationships. He is a man of God who desires value and meaning and wants to share something of himself with the world community. This is a healthy sign for those seeking second-chance fathers because it suggests that there may now be more men who can be sources of healthy masculinity and fathering. It is true that some of these men who will be second-chance fathers may carry only one or two life skills that can help the seeker along the way. It is also true, however, that we all have a natural drive for wholeness and holiness that can lead us to the ultimately fulfilling sources of fathering and masculinity.

The touch of a mother teaches tenderness and gentleness. The touch of a father teaches strength and endurance. Together they teach us tender strength and gentle endurance. The mix of what mom and dad impart to us helps to fulfill our need for life skills and fill that special place in our chest. Each parent has something unique and particular to offer us.

Moms have an emotional umbilical cord that helps them to "feel" and "read" the child from moment to moment. Mothers, for example, tend to discipline on a moment-by-moment basis. Fathers discipline by rules. Kids learn from their moms how to be aware of their emotional side. From dad, they learn how to live in society.[10]

According to the *American Heritage Dictionary of the English Language,* the noun "mother" refers to: "A female that has borne an offspring. . . . A creative or environmental source. . . . Qualities attributed to a mother, such as capacity to love." The verb can mean: "To create and care for; instigate and carry through. To watch over, nourish, and protect." According to the same dictionary, the noun "father" refers to: "A male parent. A male who functions in a paternal capacity with regard to another." The verb can mean: "To create, found, or originate. To acknowledge as one's work; accept responsibility for."[11] A historical anecdote can help to put some perspective on the importance of some of these characteristics and definitions.

During the nineteenth century, more than half of the infants in their first year of life regularly died from a disease called marasmus. This is a Greek word that means "wasting away." The disease was also known as infantile atrophy. Because of this and other diseases, as late as the second decade of the twentieth century, the death rate for infants under one year of age in different foundling institutions throughout the United States was nearly 100 percent. This so alarmed several doctors that one of them, J. H. M. Knox, did a study in Baltimore of two hundred infants admitted to various institutions. Almost 90 percent of these infants died within a year of admission. He noted that the 10 percent who did survive had been farmed out to foster parents or relatives.[12] This indicates, of course, that these foster parents and relatives were functioning in some way as second-chance fathers and mothers and were supplying something life-giving and essential to these children. This leads now to two stories: the first is about a second-chance mother and is set in an institution not too different from those studied by Dr. Knox; the second is about a second-chance father.

Old Anna: A Second-Chance Mother Story

Just before World War I, Dr. Fritz Talbot of Boston visited the Children's Clinic in Dusseldorf, Germany, where he was shown around by Dr. Arthur Schlossman. During his orientation to the clinic, Dr. Talbot kept noticing a fat, grandmother-type woman who constantly had at least one baby positioned on her hip. Much of the time there was one on both hips. Finally, Dr. Talbot's curiosity got the best of him when he saw her carrying around a feverish, measly baby and was concerned about its health. Dr. Schlossman chuckled and said, "Oh, that's Old

Anna; when we have done everything medically for a child and it still does not respond, we give it to her, and she carries it around. She has a 100 percent success rate in cures."[13]

•

Being a good mother demands intimacy. Children require trust, a safe climate of unconditional acceptance and warmth, and clear pride and approval if they are to be healthy people, capable of good parenting when they reach that point in their lives. In her book *Mothering,* Grace Ketterman explains that the intimacy a mother ought to demonstrate is composed of five ingredients:

1. Enough self-esteem to believe one is capable of giving love and worthy of receiving it.

2. The vitality to develop a variety of interests and opinions worth sharing with another and the unselfishness to show genuine interest in another's life.

3. A sense of good judgment that enables one to keep secrets, detect any lack of integrity in another, and set limits on the degree of intimacy one will choose.

4. The capacity for warmth and affection and a healthy sensitivity to one's own and the other's comfort zone in exchanging this expression. (This quality becomes extremely significant in mothering older children who may be uneasy with too much physical affection.)

5. The ability to be profoundly honest in a non-judgmental manner. Many mother-child conflicts would never develop if moms could master this skill.

Healthy intimacy demands the ability to receive and learn as well as to give and teach. Mothers who are successful find a balance between serving and giving to their children and genuinely needing love and help from them.[14]

Each of us needs the opportunity to make this physical, emotional, and spiritual contact with our mother. With this vital contact, mothers transform their children into loving and receptive human beings. These children will come to know from the very beginning of their existence that they were created to love and be loved. They are called into this world to live their dream and live life to the full. A brief parable emphasizes this: as a mother once sat by the cradle of her child, five angels approached her and proffered her a gift for the child. The first said, "I am health, and whom I touch shall never know pain or sickness." The second said, "I am wealth, and whom I touch shall never know poverty or want." The third said, "I am fame, and whom I touch shall have immortal fame." The fourth said, "I am love, and whom I touch shall have a friend in life's darkest hour." And the fifth said, "Whom I touch shall be forever faithful to his dreams and his ideals." When the wise mother heard the fifth angel, she laid hold upon his garment and besought him to touch her child.[15]

As you discover your second-chance mother, may you come to welcome the gifts she has to offer you. No one female can meet all of your unmet needs and teach you all the life skills. But each woman you welcome into your life can share with you her fluid of life and help you replenish and restore your personal life skills.

Dreams Do Come True: A Second-Chance Father Story

Like second-chance mothers, second-chance fathers can help teach life skills to a wounded person. The following story about a second-chance father was told by M. C.: "In 1962 at age twenty-two, I married and went overseas to Germany for two years with my new husband. I recall that the first week I literally said to myself, 'Put yourself in a drawer. No more silliness, immaturity; just be a good wife, obedient, submissive, and helpful.' I decided the best way to exist in my marriage was to sacrifice all my needs for the good of the relationship and for my future family. Time passed quickly.

"By 1979, I had given birth to nine children. I was exhausted and felt so very empty. I felt that there was nothing inside of me — just a big, black hole. I cried a lot, mostly at night, alone, while my family slept. I yearned to run away but could not bear the disgrace and embarrassment of not honoring my commitment to my family and marriage. It was like my outside self was kept alive to work, provide, and care for others while my inside self was all but dead, feeling empty and lifeless. I prayed a lot and hoped for relief, but I was too ashamed to ask for help. After all, I signed up for this marriage and this family.

"In 1982, something gave way inside of me. I moved with our family to a seaside community, and it was like heaven. I could *breathe* and I began to feel like a human person once again. The people of this small, ocean-side community treated me as a valuable and lovable person. I made some wonderful friends who showed me that I could laugh once again and learn how to have some fun. My husband was not pleased with the move. I was not obeying, submitting, or being as helpful as I had been in the previous years of our marriage. The black hole inside didn't hurt quite as much.

"Then in August 1983, I was invited to a dream workshop at a local retreat center. As the leader spoke, I felt life stirring in me, a sort of shift. Parts of my inner world that I had allowed to wither and die from emotional starvation were stirring within me. My heart pounded; I could hardly catch my breath. I knew I needed to listen. Somehow at the core of me, I knew it was the key to my survival.

"I wanted to learn from this teacher and healer the life skills that my own father never taught me. My biological father abandoned our family when I was three years old. I never knew what it meant to have someone around to teach me, to show me, and to let me ask questions so that I could learn and believe in myself.

"I befriended this priest. In retrospect, I realize he became my second-chance father. Shortly thereafter, I could begin to imagine how I would live life to the full. I attended every workshop he gave for a few years. It was like being fed and nourished at a deep level within me. The hole in my chest was being filled with hope, self-worth, and promises of choice-making.

"During the past five years, I have developed enough courage and self-esteem to go back to work as an obstetrical nurse. I became a perinatal bereavement counselor and also a certified lactation consultant. I have used all the skills I have learned in the various personal growth programs I have attended to enhance my life and my family's life. Instead of attending this priest's workshops, I now help him nationwide to teach what I have learned. Recently I completed a mission brought to a Third World country, witnessing to others what I have received from my second-chance father.

"I have taken myself 'out of the drawer' and am using all the gifts and talents God had given me long ago. Today, I am still discovering parts of my hidden self that have been asleep for years. I am waking up. I feel alive and full of optimism for the future. I now am able to stand up for myself, for my needs, my hopes, and, most especially, my dreams. I treasure my family and my present life.

"In the fall, I will return to graduate school to complete an M.S. in nursing and to qualify as a N.P.N. (Nurse Practitioner in Neonatal Nursing). My thirst for life and knowledge is ongoing. I look forward to 'living life to the full,' as proclaimed in the Gospel of John 10:10."

•

Earlier we had mentioned that a father — or second-chance father — can teach tender strength and gentle endurance. Clearly, M. C.'s second-chance father helped to bring out those characteristics within her. Like the second-chance mother described above, this second-chance father helped to bring wholeness and fullness to a wounded person. Those who now carry within them a long-festering father wound or mother wound can take hope, for this healing process can be a part of their future.

Notes

1. *Time,* June 28, 1993, 53.

2. John Friel, *The Grown-up Man* (Deerfield Beach, Fla.: Health Communications, 1991), 78.

3. William J. Jarema, *Fathering the Next Generation: Men Mentoring Men* (New York: Crossroad, 1995), 152–53.

4. Readers of *Fathering the Next Generation* will recognize some of the examples found in this chapter.

5. Patricia Berry, *Mothers and Fathers* (Dallas: Spring Publications, 1990), 111.

6. Ibid., 110.

7. Grace Ketterman, *Mothering: The Complete Guide for Mothers of All Ages* (Nashville: Oliver Nelson, 1991), 11.

8. Ibid., xvii.

9. *USA Today,* October 13, 1995, Health and Education Section.

10. *Time,* June 28, 1993, 61.

11. *American Heritage Dictionary of the English Language, New College Edition,* ed. William Morris (Boston: Houghton Mifflin, 1976).

12. "Old Anna" and "Marasmus," in *Clergy Talk,* December 1990 (Tomlinson Publishing Company, P.O. Box 1809, Sequim, WA 98382-1809), 9–10.

13. Ibid.

14. Ketterman, *Mothering,* 13.

15. See "Touch Me," in *Clergy Talk* (December 1990), 14.

About the Author

WILLIAM JAREMA is a psychotherapist, a spiritual director, and an international retreat and conference speaker. He holds degrees from Loyola College, Columbia, Maryland; a Master of Science in Pastoral Counseling Psychology; a Master of Divinity degree from Catholic University of America, Washington, D.C.; and a Master in Applied Spirituality degree from the University of San Francisco. He is a priest of the diocese of Colorado Springs and is the founder/spiritual director of the Society of Missionaries of Mercy, a private association of the Christian faithful, men and women, lay and cleric, single and married, dedicated to a spirituality of mercy and the healing ministry of Jesus Christ. Through the outreach of the Mercy Center for Healing the Whole Person, Colorado Springs, he and his staff provide two national programs — the National

Institute for Inner Healing, which trains men and women to become inner-healing providers and inner-healing specialists, and the Rich in Mercy Institute, which trains men and women to become spiritual companions and spiritual directors and also includes a renewal program for spiritual directors. Each program is offered in a residential and nonresidential format during the winter and summer months in Colorado Springs. Workshops and conferences conducted by Bill Jarema on how to heal the father and mother wound have been attended by thousands of participants who have found them to provide help/healing and hope. For conferences, workshops, and training programs available in your area, call 1-800-MERCY 04.